# THE SMART WAY TO BUY A BUSINESS

**AN ENTREPRENEUR'S GUIDE TO QUESTIONS THAT MUST BE ASKED**

BY
JOHN C. KOHL, SR. AND ATLEE M. KOHL
WOODLAND CAPITAL COMPANY

*Copyright 1986 by Woodland Publishers*
*All rights reserved*
*Printed in the United States of America*
*ISBN 0-939857-00-6*
*Woodland Publishers, 3007 Skyway Circle North*
*Irving, Texas 75038-3598*

# ACKNOWLEDGEMENTS

In preparing this book, we have been fortunate in being able to count on the expert assistance and able guidance of the following individuals, to whom we are indebted: Dr. John C. Kohl, Jr., Ph.D., for his help with the preparation, editing and final review of this text; Michael R. Friedberg, Esq., the Chicago law firm of Sugar, Friedberg and Felsenthal, for verifying the accuracy of the legal information herein; Ronald J. Lambert, CPA, Chief Financial Officer of Woodland Capital Company, for his counsel on the accounting and tax issues we discuss; James Erickson and Paul Coulis, friends and former business associates; Stewart D. Siebens and John B. Lane, our partners, whose practical experience in business acquisitions was a wellspring of ideas and answers; Therese M. Wessing, Company Research Librarian, and Paula McIntosh, Administrative Assistant, for their diligence in coordinating the production of this book.

Our heartfelt thanks to these fine people!

John C. Kohl, Sr.

Atlee M. Kohl

# TABLE OF CONTENTS

# INTRODUCTION

Initially the preparation of this manual was undertaken to provide a systematic and comprehensive procedure for Woodland Capital Company's internal use in evaluating prospective business acquisitions and investments. As the effort progressed, it became obvious that the resulting process could be used to great advantage by anyone interested in buying a business; it was decided to expand the treatment to cover the broader field.

The purpose of this manual is to help you work systematically through the business acquisition process. When you have carefully reviewed the several hundred questions that follow, you will have successfully addressed virtually every essential issue to acquiring a business.

Unlike many currently available publications suggesting purchasing approaches, this manual does not only concentrate on small business opportunities. The procedure outlined is applicable to businesses ranging from the small, individually owned enterprise, to the larger, publicly held corporation.

There are no detailed discussions of sources and methods of financing acquisitions, nor of possible problems following a purchase. In view of the wide application contemplated for this manual, it was decided that the inclusion of such discussions, as well as case histories as described in some publications, would detract from the straightforward analytical procedure outlined. Only brief, general comments are inserted to indicate the significance of each stage of the process.

Checkpoints at the end of each chapter, where appropriate, encourage constant evaluation of the accumulating information.

The prescribed approach, unfortunately, cannot guarantee that a purchase based on its use will be an unqualified success. Nevertheless, from the authors' operating experience, use of this manual as outlined can be a very effective way to conclude a smooth acquisition process while avoiding costly mistakes and disappointments.

Finally, we add a word of caution. There are certain issues involving the acquisition of a business that depend upon a legal interpretation of the current activities of the business and an understanding of local laws. While some legal issues are addressed in this guide, we are not implying that all legal issues are covered here nor are we suggesting how these issues which are raised here should be handled. We urge all prospective buyers to review with an attorney the legal aspects of the proposed acquisition and the documentation of the transaction.

# THE SMART WAY TO BUY A BUSINESS

AN ENTREPRENEUR'S GUIDE TO QUESTIONS THAT MUST BE ASKED

# I.  QUESTIONS FOR THE BUYER

Before purchasing any business, the prospective buyer should establish a clear set of answers to a number of important questions. Without such information, the buyer may make a poor acquisition. These initial questions can form the basis of the classic "business plan" approach to a promising enterprise.

The terms "buyer" and "seller" are used in a broad sense throughout this manual. Both "buyer" and "seller" may cover an individual, a group of individuals, or representatives of a company. However, for the sake of brevity in this section, "buyer" is referred to as "I".

*1.*  What is my principal reason for buying a business?

    a.  To own and operate my own business.
    b.  To expand or diversify my present business.
    c.  To face the challenge of "turning around" a loser or revitalizing a dying firm.
    d.  To invest as an absentee owner.
    e.  To gain tax advantages.
    f.  To make a quick profit by selling assets and liquidating the business.
    g.  To exploit a personal skill or special training or a unique experience.
    h.  To turn to profit a new business concept or technological idea currently unappreciated.
    i.  For another objective not stated above.

*2.*  What are the practical limits on price I could pay—after considering the following variables:

    a.  Cash available.
    b.  Resources that could be offered in exchange.
    c.  Availability to borrow on resources available for collateral.
    d.  Recruitment of cash-worthy partners.
    e.  Formation of a new company and sale of stock.
    f.  Arrangement of a "leveraged buyout" or other creative financing.

*3.*  What interests me about this particular prospect?

    a.  It is in a field in which I have knowledge and experience.
    b.  It looks like a business I would like to own because _____.
    c.  It would probably fit my long-range plans.

    d. It might be a profitable investment.

    e. For a combination of the above reasons.

    f. Others.

***4.*** Am I in a position to take an open approach to the purchase, or should I remain "behind the scenes" for the present and work through a confidential agent?

***5.*** How can I avoid appearing "too eager to buy" without conveying the impression that I am not a serious buyer?

***6.*** How can I assure the seller that I do not represent a competitor seeking access to trade secrets?

Note: Careful attention to questions 5 and 6 are important. A suspicious attitude on the part of the seller will adversely affect negotiations.

***7.*** Do I have sufficient understanding of and expertise in the business (both in general and in the prospect's field) to evaluate this opportunity accurately without the assistance of knowledgeable experts? Do I have the time to devote to researching, structuring the deal, and closing on an acquisition while continuing to manage effectively my existing business? Can a special acquisition committee be formed to help (consisting, for example, of my accountant, business associates, lawyers and others who may have the time and expertise to devote to the project)?

Note: If you are in doubt about the answer to this question, seek qualified advice in areas of your negotiations in which you feel any lack of confidence. Unconsidered answers to critical questions can result in unsound decisions which can be difficult and costly to overcome.

*Checkpoint:*

    How can I use this manual most effectively? First, scan the table of contents to acquaint yourself with the scope and nature of the questioning, and the order in which the information is to be developed. This preview will also be helpful in suggesting the need for particular advisors or consultants.

    Next, keeping in mind your objectives in pursuing this purchase, carefully study the questions set forth in each section.

Finally, check off every question which should be asked to gain the information needed to evaluate this prospect. The advice of associates or consultants you may have retained can be useful in selecting these questions.

*Important:* Do not omit any question for which you think you already know the answer. The seller's answer could be unexpected and helpful in avoiding trouble. The best rule to follow is: If in doubt, ask every question which might conceivably yield pertinent information.

# II. MAKING THE INITIAL CONTACT

Generally the seller is initially represented by a broker. Therefore it is very important that the buyer ascertain the authority and role assigned the broker.

The following questions establish the credibility of the broker and provide preliminary information about the prospect. If the seller is the contact, then only those questions pertinent to the business itself need be asked.

*1.* Does more than one broker have rights to represent the seller? What are the provisions of any listing agreement?

*2.* Has the seller imposed secrecy on the negotiations? If so, when can the identity of the seller be revealed?

*3.* In turn, if the buyer desires secrecy, what assurances can the broker provide that will protect the identity of the buyer?

*4.* What "first-hand" knowledge of the business does the broker have? How recently has the broker had close contact with the property and the people?

*5.* How long has the broker known the seller? Does the broker have any reason to doubt the good faith and determination of the owner to go through with the sale?

*6.* What legal or accounting documentation has the seller provided to substantiate the accuracy of the information made available?

*7.* Just what is for sale?

    a. The entire business.
    b. A division or subsidiary which might otherwise be discontinued.
    c. Certain assets such as franchises, real property, future royalties, contracts, leases, patent rights, *etc.*
    d. A share of ownership with or without a controlling interest.
    e. A partnership, either silent or active.
    f. Others interests not identified above.

8. Why is the business for sale at this time? Can the offering be considered a "distressed sale" or a forced liquidation?

9. Has the business changed ownership before? If so, when and why was it sold and at what price?

10. If the business has previously been on the market but not sold, why was there no "taker" at that time?

11. What is the asking price? Is there room for negotiation?

12. What terms and methods of payment have been proposed by the seller? At this stage, can these be considered negotiable? What conditions or existing obligations, if any, are included?

13. What, if any, deadlines have been set for completion of the sale?

14. Must all requests be channeled through the broker?

15. At what time, if any, can contacts be established directly between the buyer and the seller?

16. What is the "psychology" of the seller(s)? Given the sellers apparent frame of mind, how can I best prepare myself to deal effectively with this individual or selling group?

*Checkpoint:*

If there is a clearly indicated lack of agreement with the buyer's objectives and resources, or if there is doubt that the sale is not a bonafide offering, the prospective buyer can avoid the time and expense of a continued investigation in the deal at this point.

# III. GETTING ACQUAINTED WITH THE PROSPECT

Much of the information sought in this section must be verified by third party sources. The broker should be called upon to put the buyer in touch with sources best able to answer questions about the business' past record.

1. Under what name does the business operate; is this the same as its present legal name?

2. Where is its principal office located?

3. Is the business a _____?

   a. proprietorship
   b. partnership
   c. private corporation
   d. publicly held corporation
   e. trust
   f. other

4. How is the business best described in terms of its purpose, nature and scope of operations?

5. Can the business be classified as _____?

   a. "one-of-a-kind"
   b. highly specialized
   c. broadly competitive

6. If competitive, what is the nature of its competition? How intense is the competition regarded and where is it located?

7. When and where was the business first established?

8. What changes, if any, have taken place since then in its name, location and legal form? When and why have they occurred?

9. In the locations where the business operates, are the economic, environmental and political climates regarded as favorable or unfavorable in terms of _____?

   a. competition
   b. growth

c. labor supply
d. wage rates and taxes
e. regulations
f. other(s)

*10.* At what stage in the typical business development cycle is it? What has been its growth pattern to date? What forecast of growth is projected?

*11.* In its field of activity, how does the business rank in terms of its size as indicated by any of the various measures?

*12.* What is the business' reputation among the trade, industrial and professional groups with which it may be allied?

*13.* How does the business rate with the community (business and general public) in which it has principal operations?

*14.* If the prospect is primarily a distributor, what is its rating with its suppliers?

*Checkpoint:*

At this stage, there should be no compelling reason to drop the buying effort unless the information acquired indicates a diversion from the potential buyer's established objectives or the information acquired generates serious doubts about the integrity of those representing the business.

# IV.  LEGAL ASPECTS

Legal problems, other than those of a routine, day-to-day nature, can have a devastating effect upon the financial stability as well as the reputation of a business. A prudent buyer will make every effort to determine the extent of his prospect's legal involvements. To gain a well-rounded view, contacts should be sought with lawyers representing the business, rather than limiting them to the broker and any principal in the firm.

*1.* Who currently advises and represents the firm in legal matters? Does it retain an "outside" attorney on a continuing basis or seek counsel in a case-by-case arrangement? Or does the business have full-time counsel "in house"?

*2.* Have there been any significant changes in legal services in recent years? If so, why and when were they made?

*3.* What are the major provisions of the firm's charter, registration or license to do business? Are any of these considered to be unduly restrictive? If so, what revisions would be desirable and is any effort being made to secure changes?

*4.* In which political jurisdictions (states, counties and local areas) is the firm authorized to conduct its business? Are there any restrictions in such licenses on the transfer of ownership—if so, what steps are necessary to secure required authorizations for a new owner?

*5.* If a multi-state operation, where is the business registered as "domestic" or "foreign" and what effect do such distinctions have? For example, is the business subject to the so-called "unitary tax" in any State—if so, is the firm participating in court or legislative actions seeking relief?

*6.* What lawsuits, if any, has the firm initiated in recent years—against whom and for what claims? Of those which have been settled, were the outcomes favorable or unfavorable to the interests of the business? Which if any, are still active?

*7.* What lawsuits have been filed against the firm claiming damages and compensation for injuries resulting from accidents, negligence of other causes related to operations? Of those which have been settled, what liability has the firm suffered? Are any cases current or pending and what is the outlook for settlement?

8. Has the firm experienced any claims for product liability? Is the business covered by product liability insurance—in what amounts and coverage? What is the status of any such claims?

9. Has the firm been denied any insurance coverage or has any insurance been withheld contingent upon changes required by any insurance carrier?

10. Are any of the firm's operations seriously affected by federal, state or local laws and regulations? Additionally, are any new proposals pending which are regarded as unfair or unreasonable in their impact? If so, what actions are underway to secure reasonable treatment?

11. Is the firm subject to any lawsuits seeking compliance with such laws and regulations? Are any criminal charges involved? Who is prosecuting these cases and in which courts? How seriously are these cases regarded?

12. What, if any, civil rights discrimination or violation cases have been, and are being alleged on the part of the firm and any of its employees? What is their status?

13. Are there title disputes or mortgage provisions affecting any property which might complicate its sale? Is there any effort to clear up such matters?

14. Are there any liens outstanding against any property that might delay transfer of title? When is it expected that such liens can be lifted?

15. Are there any contracts, or informal agreements and "understandings" among those having interest in the firm, which could be the basis for lawsuits seeking to block a sale? If such exist, what are they and what is the prospect that any action might be undertaken? How are the chances for the success of such adverse actions regarded?

*Checkpoint:*

A general knowledge, including awareness of significant legal problems, of the prospect's background and current situation is essential for any further, effective probing into the details of the business. In continuing the investigation, the information derived from Sections II, III, and IV should be carefully considered by selecting appropriate and revealing questions, and evaluating the answers.

It also is to be noted that a firm which has been relatively free from legal involvements should not necessarily be more favorably regarded than one subject to frequent litigation. The nature of the business must be taken into account; a firm engaged in hazardous or generally controversial operations will in its normal course "invite" litigation—its awareness of its problems and the competence of its lawyers should be key factors in judging its attractiveness as a purchase.

# V.  FINANCIAL ASPECTS—A FIRST LOOK

A meaningful assessment of a firm's financial situation should be made only with some understanding of its general characteristics. The preceding sections are intended to convey this understanding through the information gained from the outlined questioning. It is for this reason, even though a buyer's urge "to see the books" and "get to the bottom line" is fully appreciated, that this section has been deliberately placed here rather than earlier.

Further, it will be noted that the financial evaluation is divided with a "Second Look" (Section XIV) set for an even later stage. To yield a broad picture of the prospect's financial standing, this "First Look" will be drawn from the examination of available financial statements, reports and other prepared material, rather than from any direct contacts with the firm's accountants and financial officers. The "Second Look", in contrast, will depend largely on interviews to develop the details which can complete the financial picture, and confirm or upset the initial estimates.

For this "First Look", then, it is essential that there be made available the latest financial statement, balance sheet, income analysis and annual report along with such other material as may be pertinent. In addition, it is highly desirable that copies of such material for the preceding 3 years as a minimum be furnished to provide the basis for comparisons. These sources can also be supplemented for data on numerous companies by recourse to Moody's and Standard & Poor's encyclopedic reference volumes which can be found in many libraries and brokerage offices.

*1.* Who (names and address) maintains the firm's accounts, and prepares financial statements, annual reports, tax returns. and the like—a full or part-time bookkeeper or accountant, outside accountant's or CPA's, a business service, or some combination? How long has the present arrangement been in effect? What changes, if any, have taken place in recent years—what were they and for what reasons?

*2.* Are annual reports and other financial statements certified by independent auditors? If so, who performs such service? Have any changes been made in recent years? If any, what were they and for what reasons?

*3.* What are the firm's total assets as of the latest reporting date? How are they broken down among the principal categories?

*4.* Of the current assets, how much is in cash, marketable securities, accounts receivable and in inventory?

5. What percentage of the total does current inventory represent? Can this figure be considered as within the normal range for firms of this type?

6. How much of the total is represented by investments, prepayments, and deferred charges? Of these, how much is "long term"—*i.e.*, only recoverable after one year or longer?

7. How much of the total is in accounts receivable? Is there provision for "bad debts" and, if so, does the allowance seem reasonable for firms of this type and for current economic conditions?

8. Are any intangibles, such as franchises, patents, and goodwill, shown as assets? If so, and in appreciable amount, is there an explanation of the methods used in setting the monetary value? (If not explained here, questions should be asked during the "Second Look").

9. Of the fixed assets, how much is represented by property (real estate), equipment, machinery and any special items? What are the total amounts and those less depreciation?

10. What are the firms total liabilities as of the latest reporting date? How do these divide between current and long term?

11. Of the total current liabilities, how much is represented by accounts payable, notes payable, accrued expenses payable and taxes payable? Do these amounts seem reasonable considering the character of the business?

12. Of the total long term liabilities, how much is represented by mortgages and other borrowings? Are these amounts within a range that can be considered prudent for a business of this type and size?

13. What is the net working capital (current assets minus current liabilities)? Also, what is the current ratio (current assets divided by current liabilities) and can it be considered within a "safe" range for firms of this type?

*14.* What are the current quick assets, net quick assets, and the current quick assets ratio (current assets minus inventories divided by current liabilities)? Can this ratio be considered within a normal range for such firms?

*15.* What is the total current annual income? Of this amount, how much comes from operations (sales and services) and how much from investments and extraordinary items?

*16.* What is the total annual current expense? What, and in what amounts are the principal expense categories?

*17.* What are the net earnings (before taxes), net income or profit (after taxes)?

*18.* What is the net profit ratio (net income divided by income from operations, excluding income from other sources)? Is this figure within a desirable range?

*19.* What is the current operating profit (income from operations minus expense of operations)? What is the current operating margin of profit ratio (profit from operations divided by operating income)? Does this figure indicate a satisfactory level of operating efficiency, and compare favorably to other businesses in the same field?

*20.* What is the "coverage" of current debt obligations (net income divided by interest and principle requirements) and other regular payments such as preferred stock dividends? Does it meet currently accepted standards for "safe" investments or borrowing?

*21.* What is the cash flow indicated by the latest income statement (net income increased by the amount of depreciation and amortization charged to expense during the current year)? Can this be considered adequate for the efficient and prudent conduct of the business?

*22.* From a review of the annual reports, balance sheets and income statements for the preceding three or more years, derive comparable figures with those established in the answers to Questions #3 through

#21. Are there any trends, or significant deviations evident? Do the trends show a consistently improving business, a lackluster or declining operation? Are extraordinary items clearly explained in footnotes, auditors' opinions, or other statements?

23. What is the firm's net book value—*i.e.* the total amount, as recorded on the books, of the tangible assets less the current liabilities? This item can have varying significance depending upon the characteristics of the firm; a professional firm whose value is based upon the skills of its personnel may show, for example, a much lower value than a manufacturing firm of the same size but having a large amount of plant and equipment.

24. If the firm is a corporation with stock openly traded, what has been the price-per-share performance, and its price-earnings ratio (P/E) over the period covered by the available reports? On what markets does it trade? And, if not regularly traded, is there any indication of the prices at which it may have changed hands?

25. For such stock, what dividends, both total and per-share, have been paid over the same period? Have any dividends been omitted—if so, for what reason? What is the pay-out ratio currently and how has it changed over the period?

*Checkpoint:*

If the buyer has performed his own analysis and now has any doubts about the interpretation of the figures, a review by a qualified accountant would be in order before any final conclusions are reached about the prospect's financial condition. Also, if there have been delays or difficulties in securing the needed financial information, there may well be cause for concern about the reliability of the data; in this case verification should be sought before making a final evaluation.

Should it be decided that the "First Look" indicates the strong probability of continuing financial weakness and even failure, only the prospective buyer's willingness to accept the challenge and, hopefully, achieve a "turn-around" would warrant further consideration of this prospect.

# VI.  OWNERSHIP

The role of the owner(s) can range from an active, totally-involved interest to a virtually passive concern in the day-to-day affairs of a firm. Establishing the nature of ownership is, therefore, an essential stage in evaluating a prospective purchase because the owner, as legally recognized, not only has the ultimate decision in any sale, but also may, or may not exert significant influence, through management, on the firm's performance.

This section on "Ownership" is directed to the development of detailed information about the manner in which the owner's interest in the firm exists. It is supplemented by the following section on "Management" which will concentrate on organizational pattern, key personnel and the sources and channels of authority.

Because of the complex nature of the ownership interest in a publicly-held firm, it will be noted that many of the following questions are limited to that form. Once the type of ownership is established, only those questions having direct bearing need be asked.

*1.* How is the firm owned—as a proprietorship or partnership, or as an incorporated company privately or publicly-held?

*2.* If a proprietorship or partnership, who are the owners and what are their backgrounds? Were they the original owners? If not, how long have they owned the firm? If more than a single owner is involved, how is the ownership interest divided and who exercises control? Are the owners actively involved in managing and in what way? How important is the proprietor (and/or partners) personally to the continued success of the company (goodwill, expertise, *etc.*)

*3.* If a privately-held corporation, who holds shares and in what relative amounts of the total? What, if any, are the relationships (business and family) among the owners, and how is control of the firm exercised? Are any owners active in management—if so, in what ways?

*4.* If the firm is a family-held corporation, are there any disagreements among family members which have adversely affected performance and which might seriously interfere with reaching agreement on a sale?

*5.* If originally a publicly-held corporation which "went private", when did the change take place and for what reasons?

6. If originally a privately-held corporation but now publicly-held, when did the change take place and for what reasons?

7. If a publicly-held company, what classes of stock have been authorized—and in what amounts? How many shares of each class have been released and sold, and how many are retained?

8. What are the voting rights, preference provisions, and pre-emptive privileges, if any, of the various classes of stock? Are there provisions for cumulative voting?

9. Do any shares carry an "investment letter"?

10. Are any restrictions on the transfer of any shares? Is there any limitations on their use as collateral?

11. On what markets is the stock traded? Have any shares been traded below book or otherwise stated value? How has the stock performed on the market during the past 12 months (both price and volume)?

12. Are all outstanding shares fully paid for? If not, what balances are due—when and from whom?

13. What shareholder agreements, if any, are known to be in effect and between what parties? Are there voting agreements, for example, among certain parties? Similarly, are any buy/sell agreements known to be in effect, such as stock redemption agreements or provisions in employment contracts giving rights or obligations to buy or sell shares?

14. What rights, warrants and options, if any, are currently offered? What are their terms and expiration dates?

15. How does stock ownership break down by numbers of shares and percentage of the total for each class (both actual holdings and pro-forma assuming any rights, warrants or options were to be exercised)?

16. What percentage of total shares is held by institutions and, if known, by which institutions?

17. Who owns a controlling interest—an individual, an affiliated group, or an institution? How many shares are owned, both directly and beneficially, and what

is their percentage of the total? Is such control active or passive and with what regard to management?

**18.** How is control exercised? Does the percentage of the shareholder vote required vary with different forms of corporate actions? Are there informal voting "blocks" among the shareholders as the result of, for example, family or business relationship or friendship?

**19.** Could the exercise of available options, rights and/or warrants materially affect the present control?

**20.** With reference to the holdings of any major stockholders, have any shares been placed in trusts or "gifted" in such a way that complications could arise in the event of a controversial shift in control of the company?

**21.** What is the general reputation of the owners of the firm, or, in the case of a publicly-held company, the holders of the controlling interest?

*Checkpoint:*

For the would-be buyer whose objective is the outright ownership or controlling interest in a firm, only those questions applicable to privately-held and smaller companies will probably be asked. In such instances, the evaluation of the answers might be delayed until such answers were judged along with those of the "Management" section which follows.

For the buyer who is utilizing this manual as a guide in his search for prudent investments rather than ownership, all of the questions may be pertinent. Their answers may have a critical bearing and should be carefully considered at this time.

# VII. MANAGEMENT

It is axiomatic that an effective management team is an essential element in the continuing success of an enterprise. Assessing the quality of a firm's management is, therefore, an important stage in determining the desirability of a purchase. Unfortunately, this can sometimes be difficult because apparent managerial shortcomings may be caused by undue influences exerted by owners whose current objectives do not coincide with worthy long range goals.

To obtain a realistic understanding of the structure, talents, and problems of management for the targeted purchase, this section poses numerous questions. Also included are several questions directed toward revealing the ways in which ownership can exert its influence, either directly as officers or managers, or indirectly through the board of directors representing the owning shareholders in the case of an incorporated company.

The answers to these questions must, in most cases, be derived from personal contacts with informed individuals—generally members of the firm's management staff. Persistent efforts may be needed to arrange suitable interviews and should not be abandoned until the picture is complete.

*1.* How is the management of the firm organized? What are the positions and how are they related? (Except for a very small firm, the current organization chart should be available).

*2.* Who are the present holders of the designated positions? (A listing should be furnished to show: title, name, age, education, training and prior experience outside the firm, positions held within the firm, date named to present post and salary). At what stages of their careers are they (just starting out, mid-careers, near retirement, *etc.*)

*3.* Are there currently any departures, such as unfilled or combined positions, from the established organizational structure? If so, what are they and why do they exist?

*4.* Have any recent changes in management personnel taken place—for what reasons and what positions were involved? What, if any, changes now being considered will affect which positions and for what reasons?

*5.* Are there any presently known health problems among key personnel that may be impairing their performance?

6. What "compensation-type" fringe benefits are available to officers and other managers (bonuses, company-paid insurance, deferred compensation, stock options, *etc.*)?

7. Do any officers and managers hold employment contracts? If so, who are they and what are the terms of such contracts? Are there provisions for severance pay or for so-called "golden parachutes" if the firm is sold; if so, what are the potential obligations?

8. Are officers and managers required to sign pledges to maintain the confidentiality of privileged information and any so-called "non-compete" agreements? What are the terms of such pledges and agreements?

9. In what "outside" interests (other businesses, government commissions, advisory committees, *etc.*) are any staff members involved? Who is involved and for what percent of their time? How has any potential conflict-of-interest been determined and how are the individuals and the firm protected?

10. Which staff members, if any, are presently active in trade and industry associations, and community, civic, and charitable organizations? Are such activities viewed as beneficial to the firm and encouraged—in what ways?

11. What efforts, if any, are being made for so-called "management renewal" through encouragement and provision for staff members' attendance at short courses, management seminars and institutes, conferences, and periodic leaves-of-absence?

12. Viewed as a management team, what are its particular strong points? Are there certain individuals who might be regarded as "indispensable" to its overall performance? Who is regarded as the leader or dominant member of the team—because of talent, personality, or what other quality or combination?

13. Again, viewed as a team, what weaknesses are evident? Do these stem from the basic organizational pattern, from individual shortcomings, or other causes? Are there personality conflicts and jealousies that are impairing effective management? If so, what steps are being taken to overcome these perceived weaknesses?

*14.* What is the management's reputation, as distinct from that of "the company", among its trade or industrial competition, the financial community and the public? Is any individual officer or manager regarded as "outstanding"?

*15.* To what extent is the management personnel aware of the potential sale or change in control of the firm? Is their knowledge based on rumor or formal disclosure? How has morale been affected? Are there expressed or latent concerns and opposition to the sale which might complicate a settlement or cause later problems?

*16.* Have any key people in management indicated plans to leave the firm in the event of a sale? Would it be desirable to make a special effort to retain them? What changes in the business would management, in general, like to see instituted with your assumption of ownership?

*17.* What are the ownership positions, if any, of the individual officers and managers (in the case of a corporation, number of shares, stock options, and warrants or rights)?

*18.* For an incorporated company, who are the members of the board of directors—by name, title, age, length of service on the board, business affiliations and positions, number of shares owned or controlled directly and beneficially, and the percentage of outstanding voting stock which they represent?

*19.* How are the directors nominated and chosen? Is there any stipulation or policy on "outside" representation on the board? If elected, is voting "direct" or cumulative? Do directors serve for specified terms—of what length, and simultaneous or staggered? Is there a limit on successive terms or a mandatory retirement age; are there any provisions for exceptions? Are certain officers ex-officio members of the board?

*20.* Are there formally established committees of the board? What are the committees of the board? What are their functions, and how are they constituted— are there requirements for only "outside" members on certain committees? To what extent do they supplement management functions?

*21.* What is the record of the board as a whole in management affairs—passive or "rubber stamp", or active in setting policies and reviewing actions of management?

*22.* Is the board dominated by its chairman who, presumably, owns a controlling interest? Is the chairman also the "chief executive officer" of the company and active in the day-to-day affairs of management?

*23.* Or, does management have the freedom to act independently of the board so long as it adheres to board policies? Is there any conflict between the board and management over the possible sale of the company?

*Checkpoint:*

Should the review of the answers to the questions of both the "Ownership" and "Management" sections reveal any unusual situations, the possibility of serious problems after purchase should be recognized.

One situation is that in which the founder-owner continues to manage the firm with a strong hand. Unfortunately, in some cases and particularly in specialized fields such as "high tech", the creative talents of the founder who launched the enterprise are not matched by the managerial skills necessary to guide the firm when it enters its expansion period. Its current financial record may appear as satisfactory, but underlying problems may not be fully evident until after the new owner takes over.

In another situation, a firm may be highly successful because of the winning personality and outstanding reputation, in addition to particular talents, of its owner or manager. Should such an individual leave the firm after purchase, a valuable, even though intangible asset would be lost. It could be difficult, if not impossible, to replace. Disappointing results might follow the change in ownership, and a transition period of uncertain length could prove costly.

A third and more subtle situation is that where passive ownership—individual or corporate—has allowed a management with little or no ownership stake "to run with the ball." If the new owner expects to assume an active role, resistance to any curtailment of existing management's independence could bring on a battle for control and a period of costly turmoil.

For any one of these situations, the prospective purchaser should review the objectives of buying and should consider carefully the availability of financial resources which might be needed to survive a non-profitable transition period.

# VIII.  EMPLOYEES

A major asset for any firm, and especially one in a labor intensive field, is a well-trained and stable work force. The questions which follow in this section have been designed to reveal the make-up and nature of a firm's work force along with its personnel policies and programs. Additionally, certain questions are included for the purpose of uncovering any personnel problems and circumstances which might adversely affect a firm's performance.

1. Who handles employment and other personnel matters—*i.e.*, job descriptions, hiring and firing, training, and benefits, *etc.*? Are these responsibilities centralized or variously assigned? Who sets personnel policy and exercises overall authority?

2. In hiring and firing, and in promotions, what procedures are in effect to insure compliance with Equal Opportunity requirements and other applicable anti-discrimination (including age) laws, ordinances and regulations?

3. In hiring, how are potential employees screened to determine their fitness? Are there security checks—by whom? Are any employees bonded?

4. What personnel records are maintained and what information do they cover—in what detail? Who has responsibility for compiling them? How well are they kept up-to-date?

5. What is the firm's present total number of employees? How is this number distributed (by percentages) among typical job classifications such as: skilled and semi-skilled; salaried and hourly; full- and part-time; or other categories which may be used by the firm?

6. How do the numbers derived from the preceding questions compare with the average annual figures for the current year and those of recent prior years? If there are substantial variations, what are the highs and lows, and how can they be explained?

7. Can the work force be readily adjusted, up as well as down, to changes in the normal volume of business?

For example, is extra help required on a seasonal basis, or layoffs made during slow downs? What have been the major problems, if any, in making such adjustments?

8. For the regular, full-time employees, what percent of the total number has been employed: less that 6 months; 6 months to 1 year; 1 to 3 years; 3 to 5 years; over 5?

9. How does the rate of employee "turnover" compare with that of other firms of this type? Is it considered as: average, high or low? Has turnover been a serious problem?

10. Have there been any difficulties in attracting new employees, particularly those with special skills needed in this business? Has the firm been handicapped by any lack of critically needed employees? Is there an adequate "pool" of labor in the locality?

11. How does the firm recruit new employees? Is there a formally organized hiring effort, or is it undertaken by various individuals when specific needs arise in their areas?

12. What is the firm's reputation as a place to work? Are there any apparent reasons why people might not want to work for the firm?

13. How do the firm's salary and wage scales compare with those of its competitors and with general business in the area? Are these considered average, high or low when regarded on a regional and national basis?

14. What fringe benefits are available to employees? Who may qualify? Is employee insurance coverage, for example, a "fringe benefit"? Are there sick leave plans, medical reinbursement plans, and the like? Are participating employees required to contribute to the costs of any or all of such benefits? If so, in what proportions of the total costs? What percentage of the employees are presently enrolled in the various benefits?

15. Does the firm have an established pension plan? A profit sharing plan? Who is eligible? Is participation required or optional. Are participants required to

participate financially and, if so, in what proportion? If so, has there been any significant agitation for the firm to underwrite the full cost?

16. What training programs does the firm conduct, either "in-house" or with the aid of "outside" specialists? Have any been tried and then discontinued for lack of evidence of positive results? Have any been particularly advantagious to the firm—in what ways?

17. What records of employee performance exist? Are these records adequate for documenting compliance with applicable labor laws? Do these records furnish information which may prove useful later, as, for example, in the event of an employee dispute?

18. How is employee morale rated—high, average, or low? If low, is the situation regarded as serious and what steps are being taken to improve it?

19. Does the firm sponsor any employee activities such as bowling and baseball teams, social activities for families, retirement celebrations, *etc.*? Are these considered successful in building and maintaining morale and loyalty to the firm? If not, why? What is the estimated annual cost of such activities and who has responsibility for them?

20. Are there any problems with employee dishonesty? If so, what are recent examples and how have they been handled? Are any measures currently in effect to monitor sensitive positions and discourage dishonest actions?

21. Does the firm conduct any business or operations where the loss of secrecy could create serious problems? If so, what measures are taken to insure maximum feasible security in those areas? Have there been attempts or successful efforts to breach security that have prompted changes in protection? If so, what are they?

22. Are employees aware that a sale of the firm may be under consideration? Have they been officially informed or have they learned of the possibility through the "grapevine" or rumors from outside sources? Is there any evidence of lowered morale or declining performance?

**23.** If there is such evidence, are any steps being taken to reassure the employees? Would it be appropriate to indicate, insofar as possible, the probable plans of the new owner if a sale were to take place?

**24.** Are there certain key employees so closely identified with the present success of the firm that their loss would create serious disadvantages for a new owner? If so, who are they and what arrangements might be made to insure their continuing with the firm?

*Checkpoint:*

So much of the information derived in this section will be meaningful only if considered in the light of other aspects that such information should not, by itself, be decisive in forming an evaluation of the firm. Nevertheless, it can aid in clarifying or explaining any obscure points which arise in reaching a final conclusion.

# IX. LABOR RELATIONS

Even more than employee matters, labor relations can be a highly sensitive subject. An inquiry such as this one must be conducted with discretion to maintain a neutral posture. Otherwise, both immediate and longer-range problems can be generated if the questioning conveys any impression that the potential buyer holds an anti-union bias.

*1.* Is the firm a "union shop", non-union, partially organized or "open shop"? Who handles labor relations?

*2.* If non-union, what organizing efforts have been made? When and why did they fail? Are any new attempts underway or planned? What unions are involved? What are the chances of remaining non-union?

*3.* If now organized, is the firm an "open" or a "closed shop"? How long has it been "unionized"? Which unions are represented and how many employees does each one claim as members?

*4.* If the firm operates in more than one place, are the same unions represented at all locations, or do situations differ with some even non-union? What problems have such varying situations, if they exist, created?

*5.* What demonstrations, work stoppages or strikes have occured in recent years, either as part of organizing efforts or in connection with union contract demands? How many, if any, had official sanction of the unions involved? How many were "wildcat"? Are there presently any union actions against the firm, either in progress or threatened?

*6.* Have any such events had a seriously adverse impact on the firm—in what ways? Were there threats of violence or actual violence resulting in personal injury or property damage? Were court and police actions necessary? What unions were involved and did they generate any support among sympathizers or the general community?

*7.* Are any union actions against the firm currently expected or are relations regarded as "amicable"?

8. If more than one union has representation, have there been any jurisdictional disputes among them? Is this likely to be a continuing problem, or have they been settled? Do any such settlements handicap operations?

9. How have disputes with the unions generally been settled—by direct negotiation, with a mediator or by arbitration? Are any of the unions regarded as difficult to deal with? How successful has the firm been in reaching reasonable agreements?

10. What union contracts are currently in force? If more than one, when do they expire—all at the same date or at various times? Do they include any provisions which have proved undesirable, excessively costly, or an interference with efficient operations? Can they be re-opened for renegotiation before their expirations?

11. Are there indications of new union demands which might be unacceptable? What are they and when is it expected that they may be formally presented? Is it anticipated that reasonable agreements might be difficult to reach?

12. Are contract negotiations for the firm conducted by: the firm's designated labor relations manager, some other staff member, or an "outside" labor specialist or attorney? Are outside unions and company union negotiations handled differently—in what way? Is legal counsel present in all negotiations—who?

13. Would a change in ownership of the firm be expected to make an immediate change in labor relations?

*Checkpoint:*

Harmonious labor relations are always a desirable state of affairs unless they have been achieved by letting organized employees, through their union, "run the show". Appearances of harmony can be deceiving. Reported good relations should be confirmed, assuring you that there are no underlying conditions which may eventually cause trouble. But current labor controversy does not necessarily mean a permanently discouraging situation; if the basic cause is one of clashing personalities rather than serious differences on issues, a change of ownership could be the correcting factor.

# X. PHYSICAL FACILITIES

Depending upon the nature of its business, a firm's physical facilities—land, buildings, equipment and the like—may or may not be of particular interest to a prospective buyer. Nevertheless, gaining detailed information about such facilities is an essential part of the process of evaluation. The contrast between a personal service type of business and manufacturing plant is obvious, but the service firm might have technologically-advanced equipment which could lessen any apparent difference in values.

It is strongly suggested, if it possibly can be arranged in conjunction with the questioning, that an "on-the-ground" inspection of facilities be conducted. A much clearer understanding could result.

1. What physical facilities, including those which may not be currently in use, are owned by the firm? Can a complete listing be provided to show: descriptions of all major items and groups of items such as "tools." Their locations; present functions; ages; physical conditions and estimated useful lives; current market values and replacement costs; and any other pertinent data?

2. Which facilities are owned outright and which are mortgaged or otherwise encumbered? Upon what values are the encumbrances based and what are their total amounts; how much of the various principal amounts remains to be paid off; what are the interest rates and other carrying charges; are there special terms; and is there any restriction on "assumability" in event of a sale?

3. What facilities, including equipment, are rented or leased rather than owned? For what reasons? What functions do they perform and in what locations? Who are the owners? What are the rental rates, their terms and expiration dates; do they include renewal options? If there are any options to buy, what are their terms, and are there any plans to exercise one or more?

4. Have considerations been given to "sell-and-lease-back" arrangements for any facilities? If so, what is their status? What advantages might be gained?

5. If there are facilities which are presently owned but not in active use by the firm, are they being held for

future expansion? Are any rented or leased to others—under what terms and rentals? If classed as "surplus", what attempts have been made to sell such properties; and what are the prospects for successful deals? What is the estimated current market value of these unused facilities?

6. Are any facilities deemed obsolete and ready for abandonment? If so, what are they and where are they located? Is it planned to discontinue their functions or to replace them in order to maintain present operations at existing or other locations?

7. Are there major repairs, replacements or improvements presently planned or underway? If so, what are they and at what facilities are they located? On what basis have they been justified? What is their estimated cost?

8. Are any relocations and consolidation of certain functions presently planned or underway? If so, what is involved? What are the reasons for such changes and what advantages are expected to result?

9. Are existing facilities considered sufficiently adequate and efficient to meet the projected volume of business and changes in its nature over the next five to ten years? If not, are there any plans for meeting such needs? What are they? What is the estimated cost? How would such improvement and expansion be financed?

10. Are there convenient and adequate parking facilities for employees, customers, and visitors? Do any locations have critical parking problems where there are limits to any reasonable expansion? Are these serious enough to justify possible relocations?

11. Are needs for utility services—electricity, gas, water, sewage, waste disposal, etc.—being met reliably and at reasonable costs? Can they be regarded as having capacity to meet projected needs? If not, what measures are underway to insure adequate services? Alternatively, will relocation be necessary? Who are the suppliers of these services?

12. What measures have been taken to provide security against crime and to protect property from fire and

natural disasters such as floods, *etc.*? What public safety services are available or does the firm provide some or all of its protection?

13. What and how much insurance against casualty losses is currently in force. What insurance carriers and agents are involved or is the firm self-insured? Have there been any significant losses which were not covered—for what reasons? Are there any insurance inspection recommendations which have not been followed; what are they and why have they been neglected?

14. Have any facilities or installations been found to be in violations of official building, safety or fire codes? What is the present status of any such findings?

15. Do current and anticipated operations require any highly specialized or unusual machinery or other elements for which replacements are difficult to procure? If so, what are their remaining useful lives and what preparations can be made to insure continuity of operations?

16. To what extent is the firm dependent upon reliable and efficient communications, both "in-house" and with any scattered operations such as branches and cars or trucks on the road? Are existing arrangements satisfactory—what are they? What improvements may be needed and what efforts are being made to upgrade services? Is "cellular phone service" available—is it being used or considered?

17. Are computers included in the firm's equipment—for what purposes, if any? What types are employed and how many are in use? Are they leased or owned? What problems have been encountered and have they been overcome—how? Have any studies of potential computer usage been made and by whom, with what recommendations?

*Checkpoint:*

Unless answers to the foregoing questions along with the suggested personal inspection provide evidence of inefficient, run-down or out-moded facilities, there should be no reason to drop interest in a purchase at this point. Information obtained from this stage, however, should be kept in mind during negotiations and could be useful in establishing the price.

# XI.  OPERATIONS

The use of the term "operations", often construed to cover all regular activities of a business, is here limited to the largely physical aspects—manufacture, assembly, performance of services, and the like—in contrast to the predominantly mental aspects of the "marketing" and "selling" that are the subjects of subsequent sections. "Transportation" is also treated separately insofar as it is a supporting service and not the primary business of the firm.

Several questions, it will be noted, which have appeared in preceding sections may seem to be repeated in this or following sections. This has been done deliberately because answers to such questions, when presented in a different context and drawn from a different source, can provide added information which, otherwise, might be overlooked.

1.  How can the physical operation of the firm best be described in general terms? If more than one type of operation is carried on, how are they related, and what are their relative sizes?

2.  If operations are conducted at more than one locations, how are they arranged—individually self-contained operations turning out completed units and serving particular markets, or mutually interdependent operations producing only components to be assembled at certain locations? If operations are mutually interdependent, how is the work divided and, most importantly, coordinated? What communication systems are used?

3.  For scattered operations, what studies, if any, have been made of the possible advantages of consolidation?

4.  Are there adequate sources for the materials and services essential for normal operations? Who are the major suppliers and where are they located? What do they supply? Have any sources proved unreliable—are any changes contemplated?

5.  Do any operations depend upon particular supplies which are considered "critical"—*i.e.*, could shortages or interruptions in delivery cause costly shut downs? What provisions, such as regular stock piling, have been taken to insure against shut downs?

6. Are supplies bought as needed on the open market, or under long-term contracts? For such supply contracts, with whom have they been made and under what terms and expiration dates? Are there any fixed-price agreements in effect—with whom, and are they renegotiable with or without cancellation clauses?

7. Are there adequate and reliable utility and other public services—electricity, gas, water, sewerage, waste disposal, *etc.*? Are any special requirements imposed in the operations, particularly for sewerage and waste disposal? What extra service charges, if any, are levied?

8. Does the firm generate any of its own energy—for peak demand, base load or as standby in case of interruptions in normal supply? Has "co-generation" been explored as a possible economy?

9. Have operations experienced serious interruptions because of delays in securing repair services or difficulties in obtaining replacement parts or special items of equipment? What "back-up" provisions may be in effect, and have they met such emergencies?

10. How does the firm's productivity compare with its competition? Is the present level regarded as satisfactory—if not, why and what measures should be taken to improve it?

11. Can output be readily adjusted, up or down, to meet unexpected changes in demand? Within what range can adjustments be made without significant impact on costs? How much can output be increased above the normal rate before current capacity limits are reached?

12. What is the firm's reputation for the quality of its products? Have there been problems with quality control? If improvements are needed, what steps are being taken to assure higher consistent quality output?

13. Have operations created environmental problems—smoke, fumes, odors, noise, *etc.*? Which are below "hazardous" classifications set by regulatory agencies, but still arouse community complaints? What measures are, or can be taken to curtail such "neighborhood nuisances"?

***14.*** Does the firm use or store toxic and otherwise hazardous materials? Are any of its operations considered dangerous and a possible threat to the safety of the surrounding community? Have there been official and public complaints and how are they being answered?

***15.*** Is Research and Development a part of operations? If so, what are its objectives—new products, improved processes, or _____? How large of an operation is it?

***16.*** Are any secret formulas or processes involved? How is their secrecy protected? Have there been any breaches of security? How serious could a leak be?

***17.*** Does the company validly possess all patents, trademarks, and trade names which it uses? What is their expiration? What impact will their expiration have on the company's business? Are any products or processes dependent upon patents, trademarks or trade names owned by employees? What happens if they leave? Who owns patents developed by company employees during their employment?

***18.*** How do the firm's operating costs compare with other businesses of its type? Have costs increased or declined in recent years—for what reasons? How much attention is given to cost control and what, if anything, is being done to minimize operating costs?

*Checkpoint:*

Because operating efficiency, viewed overall, is a direct reflection of the quality of management, unsatisfactory or disturbing answers to the foregoing questions should have less bearing upon a decision about buying than upon the problems the buyer might face after an acquisition. Only the buyer seeking a prudent investment, rather than control and operation of a firm, should be discouraged by the findings of this stage of his inquiry.

# XII.   TRANSPORTATION

Except in those firms whose primary business is transportation, the essential movements of materials, products and people are all too often regarded as merely incidental factors, and even virtually ignored as significant elements of success. To emphasize its importance, the necessary questions about a firm's transportation services are separately grouped in this section rather than subordinated to "Operations."

Costly disruptions in production schedules can result from failures to receive incoming supplies on time; aggravating delays in deliveries can lose customers; uncontrolled travel by executives, sales personnel and others means wasteful expense. These and other problems, such as poor selection and maintenance of firm-owned trucks and cars, can be quite revealing about the management's recognition of the importance of reliable and economic transportation services.

*1.* To what extent is transportation employed in the firm's operations? Of total operating costs, how much is attributable to transportation?

*2.* How are transportation operations handled administratively? Is responsibility divided between "outside services" performed by others and "internal" or "inter-unit" services performed by the firm's own personnel and vehicles? Who, if anyone, has overall responsibility?

*3.* What, if any, transportation services are performed by the firm itself? What equipment, by type and number of vehicles, is owned or leased? Of the owned vehicles, what are their ages; when are replacements scheduled; and what investment do they represent? Of leased vehicles, what are the annual rentals and terms?

*4.* How is the use of company vehicles managed on a day-to-day basis? Are passenger cars handled differently than trucks—in what ways?

*5.* Does the firm own or lease other transportation equipment—planes, helicopters, rail cars, boats, barges, *etc.*? If so, for what purposes? How are they managed and how much is currently invested?

*6.* Upon what "outside" services—common carriers, contract and private operators—does the firm depend? How important are they to the total operation? What are annual costs of these services?

7. Upon what basis were these services chosen—if there were any choices possible? Who made the selections? Are the rates and performances monitored by a professional traffic manager? If so, is he an employee of the firm or a consultant?

8. When changes in charges or services by the regulated carriers serving the firm arise, who represents the firm in hearings before the official regulatory agencies having jurisdiction? Or has the firm accepted such changes without entering complaints?

9. Who arranges executive and other company travel—an employee or a travel agent? Is the cost of such travel closely monitored—by whom? What is the annual cost?

10. To what extent have considerations of transportation entered into decisions on locations and lay-outs of facilities—for example, would proximity to an interstate highway interchange or a major airport have a significant influence?

11. Are there any recent studies of transportation alternatives? If so, by whom were they made and what were the findings? Were any changes made, and are any contemplated—at what cost and savings?

12. Are transportation services and operations generally regarded as satisfactory? If not, why not? What recommendations are in order?

*Checkpoint:*

Refer to Section XI.

# XIII.  INVENTORIES

Among the significant indicators of the quality of a firm's management is the degree to which inventories are effectively controlled. The amount of materials and supplies not immediately used in production, and the volume of finished products awaiting sales, can be valuable assets or costly burdens. In which category they fall will be determined largely by the skill exercised in their continuing control.

From the use of the questions in this section, it is expected that a prospective buyer will gain needed insights into the status of the firm's inventories and the manner by which they are controlled.

*1.* Who in the firm decides on the size of the stock-piles needed for the maintenance of efficient operations? Is responsibility for both production and sales inventories centralized or divided?

*2.* In making decisions, what are the more important considerations—to avoid shutdowns or slowdowns in optimum operating rates if flow of incoming supplies is interrupted, to take advantage of price changes, to minimize taxes by keeping low stocks, to accumulate unsold products while maintaining optimum operations, to permit property delivery-on-sale, or other objective?

*3.* On what basis is the size of inventories decided—by projections of past experience, by continuous analysis and forecasts of demand, by "educated guesses," or by some other system?

*4.* Are there fixed annual targets for the amounts stock-piled or are periodic adjustments made in anticipation of changing circumstances?

*5.* How are the stock-piles monitored—by manually kept "in-and-out" records, by periodic audits, by computerized systems, or some other method? Who does the monitoring?

*6.* Is the present system adequately serving the firm's needs or are changes indicated? Have there been problems and how have they been corrected?

*7.* What amounts (in quantities and dollar value) of materials and supplies are normally stock-piled before being moved into production? What are the current

amounts? Of the current inventory, how much is estimated to be in excess of presently anticipated need
and how much is estimated to be obsolete because of
changed production?

8. How dependent is the company upon any one supplier for its operation? Is that supplier financially
healthy? Are there any contracts with suppliers due
to expire in the near future? How will renegotiation
affect the business?

9. What finished-product inventories (in quantities and
dollar value) are normally stored pending sales?
What is the current inventory? Does it include discontinued items?

10. How many selling days does the normal or average
operating inventory represent? How does the current
inventory compare to this historical level? What is
the "target" inventory level?

11. To what extent are products "moved out" to distributors and sales outlets rather than being held in the
firm's own facilities? What percentage of current inventory is represented? Are these goods considered
"on consignment" or otherwise carried on the
books?

12. Is the firm's sales policy based upon immediate or
prompt delivery, or does it include a stated waiting
period?

13. If based upon a waiting period, is that policy caused
by—limited production capacity, inadequate storage
facilities, costs of maintaining inventories, or other
reasons? What advantages have been gained?

14. Can any significant loss of sales be attributed to any
lack of inventories? If so, what were the circumstances?

15. Have there been any serious problems in the delivery
of required materials and supplies? Are any anticipated in the near future? How can they best be met—
by increasing inventory or searching out new
suppliers?

16. Are there any tax advantages to be gained by maintaining inventories in particular locations? Have the tax impacts been fully explored?

17. Are current stock-piles and inventories regarded by the firm's management as in a desirable balance with production and sales? Why or why not?

*Checkpoint:*

Unreasonably large inventories at the present time, or persistent problems in their control, should be cause for concern. Unless it can be shown that they are the result of conditions which can probably be readily corrected, large stock-piles and quantities of unsold goods could well prove major handicaps for a new owner. A most careful review of the situation is warranted.

# XIV. MARKETING

The term "marketing" has various meanings in current business practice. For some organizations, it is a comprehensive label applied, as one dictionary definition has it, to the "total activities by which transfer of title or possession of goods from seller to buyer is effected, including advertising, shipping, storing and selling". In some businesses its use is strictly limited to market research and planning, while in others it is replaced entirely by "sales."

For clarity, the limited concept of the term has been adopted for this section in which the questions are intended to develop information about a firm's activities in formulating sales goals and strategies. The picture of the "work in the trenches"—the actual processes of selling—will be drawn by the answers from the following section.

As the initial step here, the buyer must determine the seller's concept of marketing and then carefully adjust the questioning if confusing answers are to be avoided.

*1.* How is the term "marketing" understood in this firm—in a total sense covering both marketing and sales; in its specialized or limited sense; or not at all but replaced by "sales" or "selling"?

*2.* Are continuing studies carried on to determine the potential for new and improved products or services; to evaluate demographic and geographic areas in which new or additional business might be developed; and to provide overall policies and guidance for the selling efforts? If not, how are such factors developed?

*3.* Who has the responsibility for such studies— independently assigned in-house personnel, temporarily diverted sales people, or outside advertising or consulting agencies? Who makes decisions which may be indicated by such studies?

*4.* In what types of markets, as distinct from individual customers, are the firm's products and services promoted and sold?

*5.* In what geographic areas are the principal markets located? What areas, if any, are outside of the U.S.?

*6.* What is the mix of products according to their stage in the product life cycle (new, mature, outdated, *etc.*)?

7. Have there been significant changes in types and areas in which the firm does business? Have changes resulted from changing circumstances within the markets themselves or primarily from shifts in the firm's policies and objectives?

8. What is the presently estimated growth potential for these markets? What, if any, factors might adversely affect the firm's share of that growth?

9. Have any new markets been identified—type and location? Are there any plans to develop them? If not, why?

10. Are the markets for the firm's products and services considered as broadly open or restricted? If restricted, in what way are they limited?

11. Does the firm have a dominant position in these markets? Is the firm's share relatively unchanging, increasing or decreasing? Are the markets highly competitive with numerous suppliers or with a few very strong firms?

12. Have the existing markets been relatively stable over time or subject to significant fluctuations in demand? How well have such fluctuations been anticipated by the firm, and who has had responsibility for monitoring?

13. Has the firm withdrawn from any market type or area—why? Are any withdrawals planned or underway—for what reasons?

14. To what extent, if any, have foreign firms "invaded" the firm's present U.S. markets? On what grounds can foreign marketing successes, if any, be attributed—lower prices, higher quality, more attractive products or packaging, intensive promotion, or _____? What has been the major impact on the firm?

15. If the firm presently has markets in foreign countries, is "doing business" relatively straight-forward or has it been unduly hampered by restrictive trade policies, regulations and red tape, or other interferences? How successful does the firm regard any such overseas ventures? Has it withdrawn or is it making plans to withdraw from any foreign market? Why?

**16.** What is the role of advertising—to gain recognition and maintain a public image for the firm; to promote the sale of products and services; or both? Who has the responsibility?

**17.** If the firm recognizes marketing as distinct from sales, how satisfactory does it regard its marketing program? Are any changes being considered? If so, what is proposed?

**18.** To what marketing and trade groups does the firm belong? Is its role active or passive? How well have memberships served the firm?

*Checkpoint:*

Because of the close relationships, it is suggested that evaluation be postponed and made along with that for "Sales."

# XV.  SALES

An art, a science, even a profession, perhaps—no matter how it may be regarded, selling is both an integral and an indispensable part of the process of finding customers and convincing them to buy a firm's goods and services in volumes and at prices sufficient to sustain and enhance the business. Without a detailed knowledge of the nature of the sales activity, along with that of marketing, an interested buyer will be lacking an important part of the information required for a sound judgement.

Obtaining that knowledge may involve considerable time and effort, depending upon the size and type of business, because several sources may need to be sought out for answers. At this stage, however, a prospective purchaser should not relax.

*1.* How does the firm conduct its selling—directly through its own outlets, with a sales force in the field, by mail, phone or catalog; indirectly through non-owned outlets, jobbers, wholesalers, distributors, manufacturer's agents, or franchised dealers; or by combinations of the foregoing arrangements?

*2.* How successful, or satisfactory, are the present channels of distribution regarded? Have any recent changes been made or are any now being studied or planned? For what reasons have changes been made or contemplated?

*3.* How is the selling organized—as a separate function, or blended with marketing, or other activities? If the firm is small and owner-managed, how much of the selling is done by the owner? Who is in charge of sales—does that responsibility extend to marketing?

*4.* To what extent is sales activity centralized in the home office? Or is sales activity largely dispersed among clearly defined territories in the field? If the latter, how are territories determined— geographically, by product line, or by types of customers?

*5.* Are sales representatives "full-line" generalists covering all customers or specialists assigned to specific items or to particular purchasers? If both types are involved, how are their efforts coordinated?

*6.* Are the present sales organization and approaches the same as originally set up? If not, what changes have been made or are being currently considered—why?

7. How many people are presently employed in sales, including management and support staff, and how are they organized—an organization chart should be available unless the firm is very small?

8. Has the number in sales been changing over the years—up, down or relatively stable? Is it regarded as adequate?

9. What qualifications are deemed essential for sales representatives? Are technical or other special backgrounds required—for all or only for certain positions; or is merely a record of sales success sufficient?

10. Have there been problems in attracting qualified sales personnel? How are they recruited and hired? How are candidates tested and trained?

11. Once employed, are sales representatives retrained— on a regular schedule, or on special occasions such as the introduction of a new line or product? What types of retraining or refresher programs are used, and are they conducted "in house" or "outside" the firm? Who organizes and conducts such programs— staff members or "outside" specialists?

12. If utilized, are such training and retraining programs considered effective—by what measures? If several different methods have been tried, which have proved most useful—or have formal programs been discarded in favor of more individual, less-structured methods? Why?

13. How are sales representatives compensated—straight salary, salary plus bonus, commissions, drawing account plus commissions or by other arrangements? Are all representatives compensated in the same manner—if not, what are the differences and why? Are any changes being considered?

14. What sales incentive plans, if any, are in effect? What plans have been tried and why is the present plan being used—if one is in effect? If plans have been tried and dropped or no plan was ever tried out, what are the reasons for the negative view? Are any now being considered?

**15.** What travel and other expense allowances are in effect and how are they controlled? Are "company vehicles" furnished—on what basis; and how is their use monitored?

**16.** How is the morale of the sales force rated—high, average or low—by the firm and by its competition? What steps, if any, have been taken to strengthen morale and to maintain it at a desirable level?

**17.** What is the firm's experience with turnover of sales personnel? Is there a typical length of service? How many are "separated" at the firm's initiative; how many quit for their own reasons? Are special efforts made to retain any outstanding performers—are such efforts successful?

**18.** When a sales representative leaves the firm, what measures are effective in preventing such individuals from "taking" their customers with them? When the departing salesman is the principal contact with an important customer, what steps, if any, are successful in retaining the business?

**19.** Does the firm have any sales contracts with individual customers? What type of contract is favored—a specified volume at a fixed price, variable volume at adjusted prices, periodic renegotiation of price or some other arrangement? Over what periods of time are such contracts in effect— does the firm favor terms longer than one year?

**20.** If sales contracts are in effect, is the firm "locked-in" to any fixed price deals? How many are there and what are their expiration dates? Are gains or losses presently being experienced—in what amounts? Are losses now anticipated over the remaining lives of such contracts?

**21.** Does the firm do any business under "private labels"—if so, with whom and under what arrangements?

**22.** Does the firm lease any of its products—as an alternative to selling, or exclusively leasing instead of selling? If so, what are the advantages and disadvantages, and is it now the intention to continue the practice?

23. Does the firm have any foreign sales—with which nations for what products or services, and in what amounts? How is such business obtained—directly, through agents abroad or with government assistance? Are foreign sales considered a long-range advantage even if not currently profitable? Why? What problems, if any, have been encountered in financing and delivering such business?

24. How and by whom are prices set for the firm's products and services? Are prices "firm" for stated periods or "subject to change without notice"—are price lists published? If any prices can be negotiated with particular customers, who is authorized to set the "final" figure?

25. Are variations in pricing permitted for special situations—such as gaining market leadership, increasing penetration in "target" markets, moving excess product inventory, and the like? Is such a policy presently in effect because its use has proved successful?

26. Are prices subject to regulation by public agencies? If so, what products and services are affected and what regulating bodies have jurisdiction? Has such regulation proved burdensome and is it regarded as "unfair"—if more than one agency is involved, which, if any, are the more difficult?

27. What are the firm's standard terms of sale—payment period, discounts, transportation charges, allowances, returns, *etc.*?

28. Under what circumstances are goods sold on consignment? Are any now on consignment; what percent of total sales do they represent? What are terms of such sales? Does the firm regard this practice favorably?

29. What are the express warranties and limitations on warranties pertaining to the company's products? Have complaints been a serious problem? How has the number of complaints varied over recent years and how many are currently being handled? How are they handled and by whom? To what extent is this a sales problem?

**30.** What advertising programs are currently being run to support the selling efforts and what mediums are used—the newspapers, magazines, radio, TV, special displays, *etc.*? Who is in charge and what amounts are currently budgeted?

**31.** Who prepares the advertising material—"in-house" staff, outside advertising agencies, or a combination? Have there been changes in recent years—if so, what changes have been made and why? Are any presently being considered?

**32.** What catalogs, price lists, mailers, technical bulletins, samples and other selling aids are regularly available? In what numbers are they circulated?

**33.** To what extent do marketing studies and sales surveys influence the planning and design of advertising campaigns? How are the results of such efforts measured? Is advertising money presently considered "well spent"?

**34.** What is the present volume of sales, expressed both in units of the principal items and in dollars? How have these figures varied over the past five years? What projections, if any, have been made for the next several years? How are past variations explained, and upon what assumptions are future estimates based?

**35.** What is the current-year, average dollar amount of sales to the "typical" customer? How many customers are there in the groups above and below the average? Are there any customers whose business is so small that they do not justify any selling expense or are there efforts to aid them in increasing their orders?

**36.** Can a complete customer list be provided? Are the company's sales dependent on one or a few customers or do sales have a broad customer distribution? How healthy financially are the company's customers? Which customers, if any, demand and/or receive special treatment? Are there "off-price" or discount schedules for any customers? If so, how are they justified?

**37.** What adverse effects might the sale of the firm have on its sales force and its customers? Has the probable sale become well known and what assurances can be given to forestall or minimize fears of change in ownership?

*Checkpoint:*

The answers accumulated in these closely related sections, "Marketing" and "Sales", must be carefully evaluated by keeping in mind the fact that the performance of "The Bottom Line" is influenced by many forces within a firm. Misleading conclusions will be reached if a rating of marketing and sales is related to the profit-loss record alone.

As just noted, marketing and sales efforts are not the only significant forces—some firms consistently prosper even though selling is neglected, while others fail in spite of obviously talented sales organizations. Thus, the prospective buyer must determine just where the true strengths and weaknesses lie throughout the firm before making any decision to buy or not to buy on the basis of his evaluation of this aspect.

# XVI. COMPETITION

A firm's competitive position is of such importance to any potential buyer that its determination warrants this independent section rather than being included with the questions on marketing and sales. To gain a more reliable evaluation, answers should be sought not only from the seller, who understandably would tend to minimize any rivalry, but also from less-biased parties. Among such independent sources could be chambers of commerce, economic development agencies, industry or trade groups, marketing consultants, and academic people in business administration programs. Other excellent sources could be competitors, and product or service end-users.

*1.* What are viewed as the firm's competitive advantages and disadvantages in its existing markets?

*2.* Is its competition clearly identified? Is it with firms offering like products or services or with those offering alternatives (plastic instead of glass, for example)?

*3.* Who are its major competitors—by name, location, relative size, financial strength, profitability and other characteristics?

*4.* Do all of these firms compete "across-the-board" or selectively—only with certain products and services, or in particular market areas, or both? If competition is selective, which firms compete where and with what products or services?

*5.* What is the firm's market share relative to its major competitors? Within the group, have positions changed significantly—some losing, others gaining— or have they remained relatively stable over recent years? For what reasons did any changes occur? Can the firm be presently regarded as a major force in the market? Why?

*6.* What changes, if any, has the firm made in it products or services, and in its marketing and selling efforts, to improve or maintain its competitive position?

*7.* Among its competitors, what changes, if any, can be anticipated in the near future? Are any expansions or withdrawals presently underway? Are any new firms likely to enter existing markets?

*8.* Is the firm's market difficult to enter due to capital requirements, scarce resources, long lead times, or proprietary techniques—or can new competitors enter easily?

*9.* Have any trends in technology and social or economic changes been observed which might threaten the firm's growth or survival over the next several years? (For example, the development of reliable and economic paper containers for milk along with rapidly rising costs of its retail distribution after WWII made the switch from the traditional glass milk bottle attractive, and virtually "killed" its production within a few years.)

*10.* If similarly-caused radical changes should occur, does the firm have the talent and facilities that could be readily adapted to provide newly demanded products or services? Can financial resources be reasonably counted upon to meet the costs of such a changeover to the new business environment?

*11.* Is the firm's competitive position expected to change materially within the next 6 months—over the next 1 to 5 years? Why and in what ways?

*Checkpoint:*

A meaningful evaluation—favorable or unfavorable to a possible purchase—can only be reached by keeping the buyer's basic objectives in mind. An emotional reaction inconsistent with realistic intentions would be a serious mistake for the buyer seeking a conservative investment, but temporarily attracted to a firm in a highly competitive, rapidly changing field of business.

On the other hand, a buyer seeking active involvement and a challenge might be even more interested in such a firm than one in a stable business earning a modest, yet consistent return.

# XVII.  FINANCIAL ASPECTS—A SECOND LOOK

At this stage, it is assumed that enough information favorable to a purchase has been developed so that an intensive inquiry into the financial details of the firm is warranted. Sufficiently well-established contacts with the seller should now make it possible to arrange for the direct questioning of those in the firm who are fully familiar with its finances. Without their contributions to clarify and enlarge upon the earlier-reviewed financial statements and reports, many uncertainties may remain about the accuracy or significance of many numbers and practices.

This section, therefore, is critically important in that the answers derived may be needed to create full confidence in a final decision to buy or not to buy.

*1.* Who (the individuals and their titles) in the firm has responsibility for "keeping the books" and the preparation of financial statements and reports, as well as any financial forecasts? What are their qualifications?

*2.* Have any changes in such personnel been recently made? If so, what were they and why were they made? Did any involve so-called "irregularities"—if so, what corrective actions have taken to insure against recurrences?

*3.* Does the firm utilize "outside" accounting services? If so, for what purposes and by whom are the services provided? Have there been any recent changes in such arrangements; what were they and for what reasons were they made?

*4.* By whom are the firm's statements audited? Have there been any recent changes in auditors and for what reasons?

*5.* How often are audits made—on a regular schedule or otherwise? What is the date of the latest audit?

*6.* What is the firm's fiscal year? Is it the same as its tax year? Annual statements and reports are prepared as of what date? Are interim reports prepared on a regular basis—how often?

*7.* Is accounting done on a cash or accrual basis? Have any changes occurred in recent years and particularly in the period covered by the statements which were reviewed in Section V? Why was the current method adopted?

8. What projections (income, cash flow, expenses, balance sheets, *etc.*), if any, are regularly prepared; for what future time periods—3 months, 6 months or longer? Otherwise, how are financing needs estimated and by whom?

9. Are copies of such projections or estimates available? How quickly can they be supplied for review? And, for a small firm without a fully-staffed accounting unit, can bank statements and accounts-payable summaries for the past 60-90 days be made available for examination; are these the basis for estimates of financial needs in the short run?

10. What is the present cash balance? How does this figure compare to that derived from the latest balance sheet, and is it consistent with any projections? How often have cash "binds", if any, occurred in recent years; is any anticipated in the near future; for what reasons?

11. What is the history of the company with respect to obtaining its financing? How do you think the financial community would view your acquisition? Would any loans, for example, be accelerated as a result of the proposed acquisition?

12. What earnings have been projected over the next several years? Similarly, what returns on equity have been projected? How do these projections compare with the actual figures for the past several years?

13. What is the current after-tax return on investment? What ROI's are projected over the next several years and how do the projections compare with actual figures over the past several years? Do the present owners regard this as a satisfactory performance and outlook for the firm?

14. With reference to the fixed assets, what are the original costs, dates of acquistion, accumulated depreciation, current value, and replacement cost of all major items?

15. What depreciation method(s) is currently used? Has "accelerated depreciation" been applied to any items and to what advantage?

*16.* What is the appraised market value of the fixed assets? When was the most recent appraisal made and by whom?

*17.* Are any fully-depreciated assets still in use? If any, what is their value and how is it carried in the accounts?

*18.* What items of a capital nature, if any, have been "expensed" over the last five years? What amounts were charged to expense? In retrospect, should any or all of these items been capitalized instead; what difference would that change have made? Does the firm routinely capitalize items in excess of a certain stated value?

*19.* What is the value of previously expensed items; if any, which are still in active use (special tools, models, design drawings, *etc.*)?

*20.* What is the value of any items not reported as assets, but currently used in operations?

*21.* With regard to current assets, are receivable accounts and notes "aged"? At what age does a receivable change from a current to a long term asset?

*22.* Does there appear to be any significant pattern showing concentrations of overdue accounts receivable? Are any customers presently denied credit because of their past due accounts?

*23.* How much is maintained in a bad-debt reserve fund? Have any recent experiences caused this fund to be increased? Is it now considered reasonably adequate or are there indications that an increase will be desirable?

*24.* What cost basis is used for recording operating inventories, and for inventory held in reserve (*i.e.* stockpiled)? If inventories are depleted, what are the potential tax problems (*i.e.* the turnaround of a large LIFO reserve).

*25.* How many times a year is inventory normally "turned"? What is the present "inventory turnover ratio"? How does it compare with any established "target" which the firm attempts to maintain? Have there been any significant variations over recent years; when and why?

26. How have the values of intangible assets (patents, rights, good will, *etc.*) been determined? Are any intangibles of possible value not carried on the books; if so, what are they and why are they not shown?

27. Are prepaid expenses and deferred charges claimed as assets? If so, what are they and what are their current amounts?

28. What investments in securities, if any, are included in the assets? What are their current market values and how much have they appreciated or depreciated since their acquisitions? Are problems anticipated in converting any of these investments into cash; if so, what items, and what problems might be expected?

29. With regard to current liabilities, what are the schedules of required payments on accounts-payable, bank loans, and lines of credit? How much is presently due and what are the unpaid balances?

30. What items constitute long-term debt? What are their amounts and the terms of payments? Do these terms include any stipulations or agreements which might adversely affect the firm's financial condition?

31. What are the items and their amounts which make up contingent liabilities? Are there commitments, such as an extended agreement with a supplier, which may be long-term; if so, what are they and how much is involved?

32. Are there contractual agreements with any personnel for bonuses, profit-sharing, severance payments and the like? If so, what are they and what is the presently estimated amount of such potential claims? What provisions, if any, have been made for meeting them?

33. If the firm has a pension or profit-sharing plan, what are its principal provisions and by whom is it managed? How is it funded and what is the current balance in the fund? What is the present unfunded liability, if any?

*34.* With what banks and other financial institutions does the firm maintain accounts—what types and current balances are carried? Does the firm have any lines of credit—with what institutions; in what amounts and for what periods of time?

*35.* What changes, if any, in financial relationships have been made in recent years—for what reasons? Are any changes presently contemplated, and why?

*36.* Upon whom does the firm depend for financial advice?

*37.* What is the reputation of the firm among its creditors? How does Dun & Bradstreet currently rate the firm; has its rating changed over the last several years—how?

*38.* If the firm is a corporation which has issued "financial paper", how is it rated by Moody's and Standard & Poor? If rated, has it been changed over recent years—in what way and why?

*39.* Are there any unsettled tax claims pending—with what agencies over what issues? What amounts are involved; are there provisions for meeting such claims should unfavorable rulings against the firm finally result? Who is representing the firm in such matters?

*40.* In addition to any unsettled tax claims, what years are open for tax examination purposes? Copies of tax returns should be obtained for all open years and analyzed for potential liabilities or refunds. Furthermore, an accountant should review the returns for "tricky" tax issues such as the availability of net operating losses, potential recapture of tax credits, and whether the company was part of an affiliated group.

*41.* Do the present owners feel "comfortable" with the firm's financial condition? Do they foresee any serious "money problems" in the near future? How would they finance growth if they were to continue as owners?

*Checkpoint:*

The answers to the questions asked in both sections of "Financial Aspects" should be carefully reviewed and discussed with qualified associates and advisors in whom the buyer has confidence.

In this way, any important omissions, inaccurate or conflicting figures, and misleading information can be more readily identified, and a basis for a reasoned conclusion established regarding the firm's present financial condition. Otherwise, such a conclusion might well have dubious validity.

# XVIII.   MORE QUESTIONS FOR THE BUYER

Although you, as a potential buyer, would not, in all probability, have reached this stage in this evaluation process without a more favorable than unfavorable view of the firm, there are several questions that you should ask yourself before making any final decision. Meaningful answers will require your recall of the principal points which your inquiry has developed. Also, such a reflective stage as this can serve to forestall an impulsive purchase which might later be very much regretted.

*1.* In retrospect, do you feel that you now have a reasonably complete and accurate understanding of the firm—its limitations and its potentials?

*2.* Throughout the process where similar questions were directed to different individuals, were there any noteworthy conflicts or discrepancies among their various answers? Can these be satisfactorily explained so as to remove any concerns which may remain in your mind?

*3.* Do you have any reasons to believe that the seller may have been all too eager to give more than the best possible impressions and is anxious to "unload" quickly his interests in the firm? Have you checked out the expressed reasons for placing the firm on the market?

*4.* Would your acquisition of the firm be in accord with your personal objectives as expressed in your answer to the pertinent question in Section I.

*5.* If not in accord with your initial objectives, is any inclination to buy generated by unexpected insights of possibilities for the firm, or is it a reaction stemming from nostalgia or similar emotional feelings? In other words, are you being influenced by superficial considerations?

*6.* All things considered, do you feel strongly that you would find ownership of the firm personally as well as financially rewarding?

*7.* Have you discussed your evaluation and inclination with any associates? Do they agree or disagree—for what reasons?

**8.** Are you now going to make a formal offer to buy the firm? If yes, can you clearly state the basis for your decision?

**9.** What price criteria (*e.g.* multiple of earnings, multiple of gross sales, multiple based on inventory, *etc.*) are normally used in arriving at a price for a business of the sort you are buying? Bear in mind the size of the business and its location as well as the industry here. Does the asking price compare favorably with that of the usual applicable "rules of thumb"?

**10.** On the basis of your knowledge of the firm, do you consider the asking price in line with its present value? With that figure in mind, what bid will you submit with your offer?

**11.** Have you checked on the availability of your needed financing so that you can propose realistic terms and conditions on which you would make the purchase?

**12.** Upon acquisition, will all the directors continue to serve? Will new directors be added to the board? What provisions will be made for liability insurance for the directors, both old and new? Do the current corporate documents provide for indemnification of directors and, if so, upon what terms?

# XIX.   THE SALES AGREEMENT

When the seller indicates willingness to consider the offer to buy and proceed with the formulation of a sales agreement, it becomes essential that the buyer, working closely with his attorney and accountant, makes certain that numerous details are included in addition to the usual price, terms and conditions of the sale.

By selecting from the following list those questions applicable to this firm's situation, and by getting clearly stated answers which can be incorporated into the agreement, there should be a materially lessened risk of misunderstandings that might complicate and delay the settlement, or even lead to litigation.

The following questions are not intended to provide comprehensive legal advice in reaching a sales agreement, and an attorney should be consulted.

*1.* Who is authorized by the seller to negotiate the price, the terms and conditions of the sale, and the sales agreement? Who will sign on behalf of the seller and what actions are necessary to authorize the signing?

*2.* What terms of sale and method of payment will the seller consider—all cash at closing, an initial payment with seller financing the balance, an exchange of property or securities, or some other arrangement?

*3.* What "earnest money" will be required? What protection will be afforded the buyer in the event of his failure to obtain any expected financing?

*4.* If an exchange of stock is deemed feasible, on what basis will the trade be executed? What provisions can be made if 100% of the stock is not immediately available for transfer because it has been pledged, placed in escrow, or declared "missing"? How will any taxes involved in such a transfer be handled?

*5.* If tangible assets (real estate or other property) are to be transferred, who will be responsible for providing security during the transition?

*6.* If the seller has tax considerations arising from the sale, what special provisions will be required? Similarly, you, the buyer should be aware of the tax advantages, such as the deductibility of the payment for certain items, in the purchase of the business.

7. What, precisely, is being sold? Are all items adequately identified and described? What items, if any, remain with the seller?

8. Does the seller's asking price include any amount representing the value of the firm's name, image or goodwill? If so, how much is it, and on what basis was the amount established?

9. What is the mutually agreed-on price? What procedures will be followed to adjust that price in the event of unanticipated changes in the condition of any items or the addition or withdrawal of items prior to closing?

10. What debts, leases, contracts or other obligations are to be assumed by the buyer? When will the seller furnish a sworn statement listing the firm's creditors and the amounts due each one as of the date of the closing?

11. What expenses, if any, which are not identified on the financial statements, become obligations of the buyer and should be listed in detail?

12. What contingent liabilities exist? How are they to be treated?

13. What provisions are to be included to cover the handling of bad debts?

14. What warranties regarding the accuracy of the firms financial statements are to be made part of the sales agreement, or furnished prior to the closing in a form acceptable to the buyer?

15. How are currently applicable taxes to be allocated between the seller and buyer as of the closing date?

16. Prior to the closing date, when can the seller's federal, state and local tax returns be made available to the buyer for review?

17. What provisions can be made for the satisfaction of any tax delinquencies that will remain obligations of the seller?

*18.* By what date will official confirmation be furnished to show that all withholding taxes (income, social security and any others) are currently paid up?

*19.* What indemnification will be granted to the buyer, and by whom, for any assessments of additional taxes due on presently unaudited returns?

*20.* Will the seller accept a note from the buyer in an amount needed to cover certain specified contingent obligations of the seller, and payable upon their satisfaction?

*21.* What parties must authorize the signing of the sales agreement on behalf of the seller? Are absentee owners involved, or in the case of a corporate seller is a vote of shareholders required? Who will sign for the seller?

*22.* What are the legal requirements for registration and publication of any notice of sale, and who has responsibility for meeting them?

*23.* Will the sale be contingent upon the purchaser's securing any required permits or licenses?

*24.* When and where will the closing be held? Who is to be present to represent the parties to the sale?

*25.* Who has the responsibility to notify, by registered mail, all known creditors of the transfer of ownership?

*26.* If contracts with suppliers have been in effect, who has the responsibility for their notification of the change of ownership?

*27.* Will the seller agree not to establish a similar, competitive business within the firm's present territory for a mutually determined period of years in the future? Will he agree not to do so within a territory where the firm plans expansion? Can a reasonable, enforceable non-competition agreement be drawn up?

*28.* Will the seller be willing to assume a consulting or advisory role with the new owner to facilitate a smooth transition? If so, what arrangements would be mutually agreeable?

**29.** If any broker's fees are to be paid, who is responsible? Seller? Buyer?

# FINAL COMMENTS

The signing of the sales agreement will mark the completion of a systematic process which should have yielded, if objectively followed, an evaluation of the firm now being acquired. If the "right" questions were asked, honest answers gained and clearly understood, there should be little reason to doubt that this is a prudent purchase.

After the acquisition is completed, however, the new owner, aided by the knowledge gained in this pre-purchase study, must exercise the necessary managerial skills to achieve the long-run goals. A successful future for a firm is not guaranteed by a prudent purchase alone.